THE COUNTRY CRAFT SERIES

PRESSED
FLOWERS

PRESSED
FLOWERS

CRESCENT BOOKS
NEW YORK • AVENEL, NEW JERSEY

This 1994 edition published by Crescent Books,
distributed by Random House Value Publishing, Inc.,
40 Engelhard Avenue, Avenel, New Jersey 07001.

Random House
New York • Toronto • London • Sydney • Auckland

First published in 1992
Reprinted in 1993
Reprinted in 1994

Publishing Manager: Robin Burgess
Project Coordinator: Lynn Bryan
Project assistant: Jenny Johnson
Editor: Dulcie Andrews
Illustrator: Carol Ohlbach
Photographer: Andrew Elton
Designer: Kathie Baxter Smith
Typeset in the U.K. by Seller's
Produced in Singapore by Imago

Title: Country Crafts Series: Pressed Flowers
ISBN: 0 517 10255 2

CONTENTS

INTRODUCTION

The popularity of creating a beautiful craft by hand is increasing among people of all age groups.

Through this Country Craft series, it is our hope that you will find satisfaction and enjoyment in learning a new skill. In this case, how to press flowers. Be it a bouquet from a special occasion, or just a single bloom, the pleasure of a pressed flower is eternal. Pressing flowers is an easy craft to learn, as you will discover.

Opposite: A colorful mixture of pressed flowers is ready to be framed.

GETTING STARTED

THE CRAFT of pressing flowers requires patience and a creative eye. From decorated notepaper to framed compositions of pressed blooms, this is a craft which preserves the beauty of one of nature's most transient delights – the flower.

The craft is based on a simple concept; fresh flowers are collected and are then pressed between sheets of paper so that their moisture is absorbed. The dried, pressed specimens last indefinitely and in this form can be included in a variety of handicrafts.

People have always been fascinated by the perfection of the flowering plant and for hundreds of years the practice of pressing flowers and leaves has been used as a way of preserving their colors and forms long after the natural blooms have faded.

Like all crafts, this one has been subjected to the whims of fashion. The Victorians, for example, had a passion for pressed flowers. At this time, the craft reached dizzying heights as people went to extraordinary lengths to create increasingly elaborate pressed flower compositions. Often, embellishments such as beads, sequins and feathers were used.

The contemporary approach is a return to simplicity, where the beauty of the blooms is the feature. As with most cottage crafts, the simplicity of the finished article is part of its appeal.

Remember when starting off that while pressing flowers and leaves is an excellent way to preserve them, their colors and shapes are altered in the process.

A pressed flower no longer has three dimensions. It is flat and therefore two-dimensional. The pressing process alters colors significantly, sometimes intensifying, sometimes reducing them. Some pressed flowers change color altogether, while in others, aspects such as a colored center are revealed.

A pressed bloom will never be exactly the same as its fresh counterpart and an understanding of this within the framework of the craft is crucial. Before attempting work on a composition or craft project, it is a good idea to spend several hours collecting and pressing various specimens and observing the results. Trial and error is an important part of the learning process and, if you are hoping to create a certain look with your work, you will be able to make the best selections from the start and avoid disappointment.

Since pressing flowers is a craft which requires careful attention to detail, clear a space in which to set out your equipment where you can work uninterrupted.

You will need good light. Daylight is best. If it is not possible to work near a window, a small desk lamp with direct downlight will help. Good ventilation is important. Any hint of dampness can lead to mildew, which destroys pressed plant material.

Flowers become two-dimensional and some change color during the pressing process; compare the pressed larkspur (right) with the fresh specimen.

Pictures are one of the most popular uses for pressed flowers. This colorful collage, composed

on a black background, has been framed without a mount. The result is quite spectacular.

TOOLS AND MATERIALS

THE TOOLS AND EQUIPMENT required for pressing flowers are simple and easy to obtain. The essential piece is a flower press and there will be a little more detail on this later in this chapter. Other equipment needed includes a selection of craft and stationery items, all of which are inexpensive.

Forceps and/or tweezers are vital for handling the blooms. Tweezers with a blunt edge help avoid the risk of piercing or damaging blooms and backgrounds while arranging pressed specimens for a composition. Forceps or sharp tweezers make handling a little easier but using these require extra care until you become adept.

A magnifying glass is particularly useful when dealing with tiny elements such as seed heads or small, delicate flowers. You will also need orange (manicure) sticks or toothpicks for applying glue to the flowers.

It is a good idea to buy blotting paper for the flower press in bulk so that you always have plenty on hand. Layers of newspapers can be used as well, and household tissues are absorbent and useful as an extra layer in the press. They are also invaluable when cleaning away excess glue or fragments of dust or dried plant material.

A scalpel or craft knife is useful and can be bought from a craft store or artists' suppliers.

A small sponge, a compass and templates for drawing specific shapes are optional.

It is always a nice idea to sign your composition and a very fine marker pen is best for this. Some works, such as samplers or country herbals, require labeling or plant identification and, again, the finest of pens is the best tool. Colored inks can be used but darker colors are more easily read. If you want to draw a border around your picture, a thicker pen will provide the best results.

TOOLS & EQUIPMENT
Flower press
Background paper
Tweezers and/or forceps
Rubber-based glue
Clear craft glue
Ruler, No. 2 pencil, eraser
Small paintbrush
Scissors, large and small
Scalpel or craft knife
Magnifying glass
Orange (manicure) sticks
Blotting paper
Masking tape
Fine marker pen

OTHER MATERIALS
Newspaper
Tissues
Sponge
Compass
Manila envelopes
Florist's shears
Templates

Background papers

The type of work you plan to do will determine the materials needed. If you plan to decorate stationery, for example, then you will need to get in stocks of good quality paper and poster-board. Recycled papers are becoming more widely available and are an excellent idea, helping to create a slightly rustic look as well as being environmentally sound.

If you plan to create compositions of pressed flowers for framing you will need to consider background papers seriously. There are many types of paper and posterboard available and your choice will have an important bearing on the finished item.

The color and texture of the background paper you choose for a pressed flower composition will have an important bearing on the finished work. This selection includes a handmade paper.

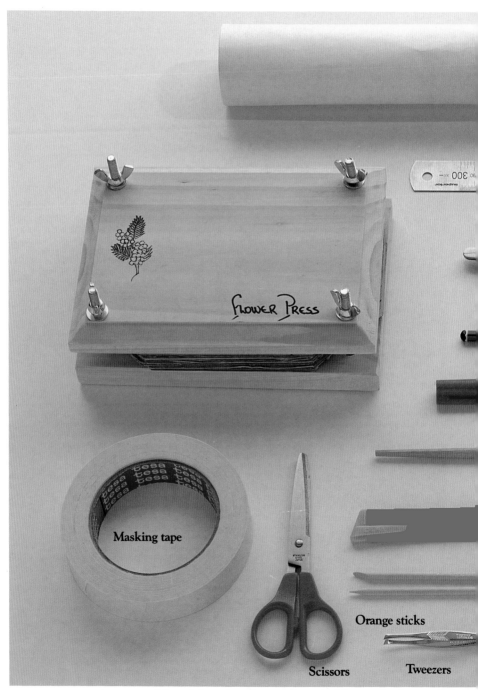

FLOWER PRESS

Masking tape

Scissors

Orange sticks

Tweezers

Most of the tools and materials required for pressing flowers, including

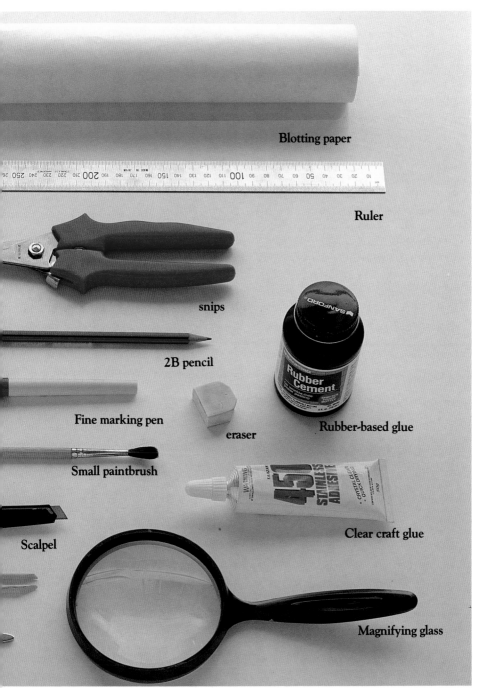

Blotting paper

Ruler

snips

2B pencil

Fine marking pen

eraser

Rubber-based glue

Small paintbrush

Clear craft glue

Scalpel

Magnifying glass

a basic flower press, are available from artists' suppliers and craft stores.

Artists' suppliers are the best source for backing paper, but you may have to look further for specialty or unusual papers. Craft suppliers usually carry stocks of papers too.

Papers vary not only in color and texture but in weight. Generally, heavier posterboard or paper is best for large compositions and larger specimens. Lighter weight papers are fine for less elaborate compositions.

Various types of fabric can be used as a background as well. Black velvet is a favorite, as are damask and linens. Remember that creating pressed flower pictures on fabric backgrounds requires a little more care, since the fabric will be inclined to move or wrinkle more than paper or posterboard and will probably need to be stretched slightly when framed.

Flower presses

The flower press is your most important piece of equipment and, if you plan to get involved in the craft on a regular basis, it is worth buying or making one.

At the beginning you can improvise by pressing blooms between the pages of a book weighted with heavy objects, or using two pieces of plywood and several bricks as a temporary press. A good basic press, however, will help make your work more professional and more pleasurable.

Fabrics such as velvet, linen, and damask can be used as a background for pressed flower pictures. To avoid wrinkling, the fabric should be stretched or fixed to a pre-cut backing board.

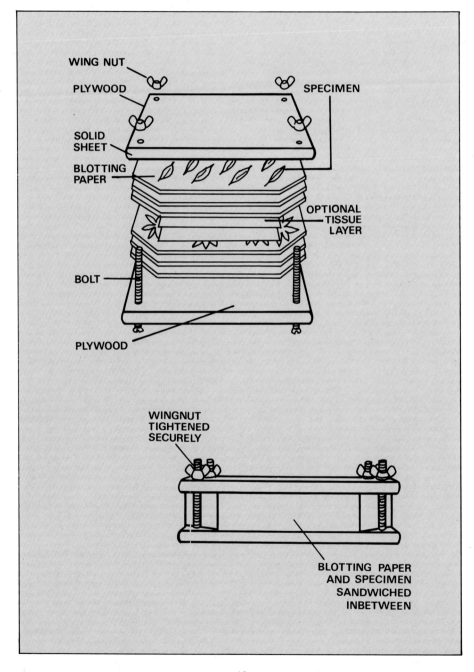

WING NUT

PLYWOOD

SPECIMEN

SOLID SHEET

BLOTTING PAPER

OPTIONAL TISSUE LAYER

BOLT

PLYWOOD

WINGNUT TIGHTENED SECURELY

BLOTTING PAPER AND SPECIMEN SANDWICHED INBETWEEN

A' basic flower press is comprised of two pieces of plywood cut into a rectangular shape. The plywood should be of a reasonably heavy gauge to withstand wear and tear. The pieces are joined with six bolts and wing nuts, one at each corner and two on either side.

To operate the press, the wing nuts are removed, the top piece of plywood taken off and the press loaded with specimens, carefully arranged between layers of blotting paper. When the press is full, the top piece of plywood is replaced and the wingnuts screwed into place and gradually tightened over a period of time to exert sufficient pressure to press the flowers sandwiched in between.

If you do not have the facilities for making your own, flower presses are available from craft suppliers and some specialty stores. If you eventually take up the craft in a serious way, you can invest in a professional flower press which works by means of a central screw mechanism. These are much bigger and easier to operate than the type of press we have described here and will enable you to press a greater variety of plant material more quickly.

When your press is not in use, make sure it is completely cleared of all fragments of plant material and stored, with the wing nuts loosened, in a well-ventilated place. A good circulation of air prevents dampness which can lead to the growth of mildew and fungi.

Picture frames

If you are planning to create pressed flower pictures, they will require framing to show them to their best advantage.

Professional framing for a lot of pressed flower pictures could prove a costly exercise, so it is worth considering a do-it-yourself approach.

There are a number of options. The easiest method involves purchasing a do-it-yourself framing kit such as those available from specialty framers and some hardware stores. Photo frames from photographic suppliers are another possibility. Or you can buy ready made lengths of frame and cut them to your own specifications.

Glass is essential to protect the delicate plant material. Non-reflective glass will help cut down on the ultra-violet rays which hasten fading, but may result in loss of picture detail.

The mount you choose helps center a work, separating it from the frame and drawing the eyes to the detail and color of the composition.

Because plants – even pressed flowers – are bulky compared to a print or painting, the frame must be deep enough to accommodate this. A professional framer will make the appropriate allowance, and you must, too. A small piece of plywood placed at each corner of the mount before the frame is added should prove adequate.

Opposite: The composition of a basic flower press showing the various layers required for correct loading (top) and the fully loaded press in the closed position (below.)

A wonderful choice of precut frames is available to complete your pressed flower picture.

This selection includes country-style timber and laminated, as well as marbled, frames.

A flower garden filled with a variety of blooms, such as this one,
provides a constant supply of fresh specimens.

STARTING WORK

COLLECTING your own plant material is one of the most delightful elements of this craft. You can gather flowers from your own yard or elsewhere, or even plan a special expedition to the countryside to pick wildflowers. City-dwellers do not have to be limited to making selections from their local florist – although this provides a wealth of seasonal material – even a balcony garden or windowsill herb garden can provide sufficient material for small-scale projects.

If you are limited to purchasing your plant material rather than gathering it, try to go to the source of supply – the flower markets. In most areas these are held early in the morning. The range of flowers is large and you may be able to buy leftover bunches at reduced prices at the end of a morning's trading.

Plants and flowers are at their best in the morning so pick them after the early morning dew has dried. Seasonal blooms should be gathered early in the season rather than at the end of their flowering cycle.

Bear conservation in mind when you gather raw materials to press. Take only as much as you need, as you would from your own yard. Do not pick blooms and leaves indiscriminately and be most careful to leave buds and shoots intact.

Botanical gardens and national parks are strictly out of bounds as they contain many protected species. In some parks and gardens you may be prohibited from removing fallen blooms, too. It is always wise to check before taking anything from these areas. Many wildflowers and native plants are grown commercially and are available through florists when in season.

As your skills progress, so too will your knowledge of what to pick. Initially, it is a good idea to gather a wide variety of plant material – leaves, flowers, sprays, as well as individual blooms, seed heads, flowers with stems intact, grasses and even weeds. Charming compositions can be created from plants commonly thought of as weeds – dandelions, common daisies and buttercups for example, or ferns and ivy. All of these can be pressed successfully.

When selecting leaves and flowers for the press, make sure they are as near to perfect as possible. Flowers should be undamaged and without any browning on the edges of the petals.

All insect life must be removed from the plant. Check carefully on the undersides of leaves and inside flowers (as much as you can without damaging the bloom) for any signs of life. Some tiny species may escape your notice at first glance but it is essential to locate them and remove them. If they are left, insects which feed on flowers can continue to do so during the early stages of pressing and blooms may emerge damaged.

Flowers should be pressed as soon as possible after picking. If you are out in the country,

Pansies and lavender are ideal plants to press.

place your plant material in a plastic bag, taking care not to overfill it. If you can, separate specimens into some sort of order as you go –herbs in one bag, leaves in another, buds in another, and so on. Some air in the bag will help protect the plants. If, on arriving home, the blooms appear to have wilted, place the bag in the refrigerator for an hour or two to help them revive.

A basic botanical knowledge of the flowering plant will prove a useful asset to this craft and there are any number of books on the subject. A general understanding of the growing cycles of various plants will help you know when is the best time of year to gather or buy specimens, while a knowledge of the structure of the flower itself will help when it comes to specific pressing techniques such as pulling flowers apart and "reconstructing" them. (This will be discussed in more detail

in the next chapter.)

It is important to keep an open mind when gathering plants for pressing. Some of the prettiest blooms in their natural state do not press as well as some of the simple flowers.

Color changes are the most variable factor you will have to contend with. All plants will look different after pressing and, while there are no rigid rules, the following guidelines are worth remembering.

COLOR	EFFECT
WHITE	*tends to become off-white or cream*
BLUES	*tend to become deeper*
PINKS	*tend to fade to a lighter shade*
GREENS	*tend to be subject to most variation*
REDS	*tend to become more intense*
YELLOWS	*tend to become a shade darker*
ORANGES	*tend to look brighter*

The pressed specimen (right) placed alongside a fresh specimen of the same species provides an excellent example of the color changes which can occur during pressing.

PLANTS FOR THE BEGINNER'S PRESS

FLOWERS	LEAVES	HERBS
DAISIES	IVY/MOST SPECIES	LAVENDER
LARKSPURS	MAIDENHAIR FERN	FENNEL
ROSES/ROSE BUDS	ASPARAGUS FERN	SWEET BASIL
ANEMONES	SHIELD FERN/FRONDS & LEAVES	MARJORAM
PANSIES	EUCALYPTUS LEAVES	PARSLEY
STATICE	HOLLY	BAY LAUREL
HYDRANGEA	MAPLE LEAVES	CHAMOMILE
FUCHSIA	SEEDED GRASSES	SAGE

TECHNIQUES OF THE CRAFT

PLACE PLANT MATERIAL in the press as quickly as possible to insure good results and the best possible colors in the pressed specimen. Speed at this stage also minimizes damage to blooms.

The longevity of pressed flowers is brought about by the extraction of moisture during pressing. To achieve maximum absorption, flowers should be placed between several sheets of an absorbent material such as blotting paper or newspaper plus several layers of tissues. As the press is screwed down tight, the flowers sandwiched in between are flattened and their moisture content absorbed by the material above and below them.

To load the press, cut several sheets of blotting paper to the same size as the press. Lay three or four sheets of paper to form a base. Arrange the fresh specimens carefully on another sheet of blotting paper, allowing a little space around each one. If you wish, you can lay a protective layer of tissue over the flowers before placing another sheet of blotting paper on top. Continue in this way, layering flowers and paper, until the press is full. Do not overload the press.

It is a good idea to keep plants in groups if you can; a sheet of daisies, for example, or a sheet of ivy leaves. This not only insures even pressure in the press but reduces handling of the specimens after pressing and makes their storage easier.

Fig. 1

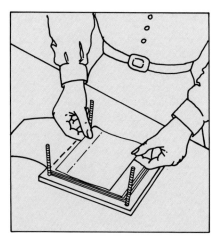

Fig. 2

Once the press is loaded, screw it down as tightly as possible. As the bulk reduces during the following days, continue tightening the press by screwing down the wing nuts or increasing the amount of weight on top.

Bulkier plants require more pressure than delicate ones. Ideally, the two should not be placed side by side on the same sheet of paper as this can result in uneven pressure and an unsatisfactory result.

Flowers should be left in the press for six weeks. You can check their progress every now and then – the relative dampness of the blotting paper will give you some indication of how things are going – but it is recommended that you leave all specimens for at least six weeks.

Some experts advise changing the top sheet of absorbent paper regularly throughout the pressing process. Others feel this is unnecessary except in the case of particularly moist plant material such as succulents. Again, trial and error is your best guide. For beginners, try changing the paper every few days at first, taking care not to dislodge the blooms. Work out your own rules as you become familiar with the procedure.

Once satisfied that the flowers are well pressed, you must also be quite sure they are completely dry before taking them out of the press. Specimens should be gently loosened from the sheet of blotting paper before being stored.

You will need some sort of storage system for your pressed specimens. A flat, plastic stacking unit such as those available from most stationery stores is deal, but a series of large manila envelopes kept flat in a carton

1 & 2 (from left to right): Arrange fresh specimens on a sheet of blotting paper and place on base layer. Place a protective tissue layer between the specimens and the next layer of blotting paper.
3 & 4: Keep plants in specimen groups if possible. Continue layering paper and specimens in this way until the press is full. Do not overload the press.

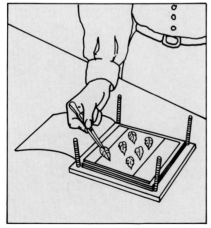

Fig. 3

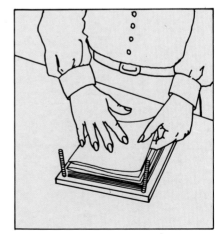

Fig. 4

will do just as well. Take care to label env-elopes or sheets accurately, not forgetting to add the date.

One of the cardinal rules of this craft is never to throw anything away. Even parts of a plant which have been damaged in the press, or broken apart during handling, may eventually find a place in a future composition. For the same reason, it is a good idea to press all the parts of a plant. Rather than separating the flower and discarding the leaves, stems and buds, press these too and store them for possible use later on.

Always press more than you think you are going to need. Even if a single bloom is all you require for a project, press several so that you have some in reserve in case the specimen gets damaged during handling. This is parti-cularly important for plants which have a very short flowering season. If you are working on a composition based on spring-flowering bulbs, for example, and run out of flowers, you will have to wait an entire year before being able to supplement the material.

Special techniques
While in most cases, flowers, leaves and grasses are loaded into the press as you see them, there are some plants which will not press successfully because of their bulk or shape. In cases such as these, specimens can be pulled apart, the various parts pressed

Opposite: Individual flowers respond quite differently to pressing.
This selection of pressed specimens shows the various characteristics of eleven different species.

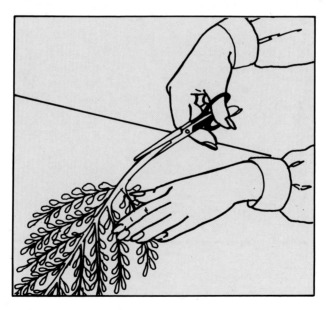

If bulky plant material proves difficult to press, trim away excess parts such as the lower end of the stalk using sharp scissors.

individually and the flower "reconstructed" after pressing. Plants can also be cut into two sections which are placed together again after pressing, or you may find that the cross-section reveals an interesting center which can add another dimension to your work.

The use of cross-sections is a deliberate device employed by many pressed flower artists, as is the use of individual petals, stems and even the smaller parts of the flower such as the stamen.

Another device you can use to create a different effect is to press flowers that are closed or partly open by carefully laying some petals back and others forward. This works very well if you are using several blooms from the same species, as it allows you to capture the full range of the plant's flowering cycle.

Tricks such as this can be used for damaged specimens too. Petals can be replaced using a touch of glue, a broken stem can be repaired in the same way and in some instances, where leaves, stems and blooms have been pressed separately, it is possible to reconstruct the entire plant.

Color enhancement is another useful technique. While in most cases a flower's natural color (even those which change or

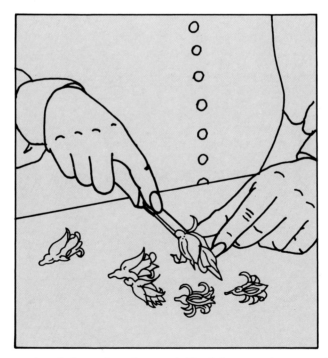

Fleshy flowers such as the hyacinth can be cut in half and then pressed. Use a scalpel to insure the bloom is cut cleanly. Once pressed, the two halves can be used individually or placed together to form a complete flower.

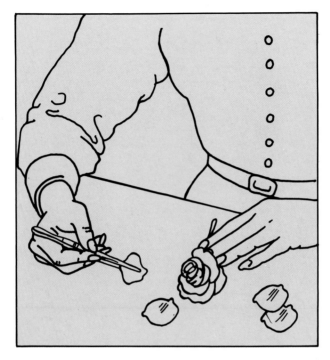

Flowers which prove difficult to press because of their size or shape can be carefully pulled apart, the various parts pressed separately, then the plant can be reconstructed.

fade in the press) is the most desirable, there are instances where color can be boosted for an effect. Certain plants are renowned for color loss after pressing; lavender is one, freesias are another.

The most effective way to add color to pressed flowers is with spray-on color and specialty florist's spray color packs are available in a wide range of hues. Used sparingly, color enhancers can add depth to a composition. Too much will give your work an unnatural look. You will soon learn which flowers respond to the addition of color and which are best left *au naturel*.

FINISHING TECHNIQUES

USING THE FLOWERS you have pressed in a project is the ultimate objective of this craft and there are many attractive projects from which to choose. The traditional ones include pressed flower pictures, which can take on many forms; pressed flower stationery, where simple combinations of pressed specimens are used to decorate notepaper and cards; and pressed flower decorations, where blooms are used to embellish items such as photograph frames, little storage boxes and so on. (Getting started on projects such as these will be discussed in more detail in the final chapter). While quite different from one another, all of these projects rely on your own creativity and it is this stage which is the most satisfying and enjoyable.

There are basic pointers relating to composition which can be followed, but your own interpretation of color, form and style will prove most important to the finished work.

SIX ESSENTIALS FOR COMPOSITION

BALANCE	SHAPE
COLOR	MOOD
TEXTURE	STYLE

Balance   The best way to arrange an attractive composition is to move your selection of blooms carefully around until you achieve a pattern that pleases you and appears balanced. The easiest way to do this is to create a focal point using a central bloom. Select a relatively large specimen for the focal point and, from here, work up and out using either curves, straight lines or any similar device which helps create the feeling of movement. Your aim is to take the eye from the center of the composition outwards to embrace the whole.

Note: Turning an arrangement upside down is a useful trick to check the balance of a composition.

Color   This is the essence of most art forms and it is the most important element in creating impact. The primary colors of red, yellow and blue are the brightest in the spectrum. Used together they create impressions that are cheerful, dramatic and vibrant. Secondary colors such as green, violet and pink are softer. Used together they convey an impression that is soft and romantic. Black and white are used for contrast and the darker colors such as browns and grays help create mood within a group of brighter hues. You

Opposite: A pressed flower circlet makes a delightful country-style craft project. Use a compass to draw a perfect circle lightly onto your background paper and let a little of the background show through between the flowers to give the composition a lighter feeling.

will find that the softer colors harmonize more easily with one another than the stronger colors and beginners may find it easier to work on a project based on one color group at first. If pressed specimens have been stored according to their color, this will make your task a lot easier. As you become more familiar with the way various colors work together you can experiment with more unusual combinations.

Texture   Since pressed flowers have been reduced to two-dimensional objects, the element of texture takes on a special importance. By using different textures in a composition, you add visual interest and help add dimension and a sense of scale. Pressed flowers with a smooth or even texture are possibly the commonest and usually form the basis of a composition. Specimens such as seeded grasses, spiky leaves and taller flowers can be used to add a coarser texture and provide vertical lift, while seed heads, sprays of plants such as baby's breath and spreading fern fronds provide softness and an impression of horizontal movement.

Shape   Since you will be working with a variety of shapes, great care must be taken in the placement of blooms to achieve an overall shape which does not overwhelm the eye. As a starting point, it is a good idea to follow the shapes florist's use when working with fresh flowers, such as posies, bouquets, wreaths and garlands. By tradition, these shapes work to show the blooms off to best advantage so it makes sense to follow similar principles when working with pressed flowers.

As you develop your own style you may wish to deviate from traditional ideas but, for the beginner, a posy of pressed flower blooms following a color theme on a plain background paper makes a charming project. Contrary to expectations, the simplest shapes present a higher degree of difficulty to arrange than more crowded compositions. The latter allows room for error, whereas arrangements featuring individual plants need to be perfect in every detail.

Mood   As color is one of the most crucial elements when considering the mood of a pressed flower project, first select your color theme, such as pink, blue or gold, then work to create a mood with those colors. Yellow, for example, combined with clear green and a little red or blue will create a cheerful and bright composition. However, combined with pastel colors, white and soft greens, the effect is different. Remember that the background you choose will have a profound effect on the mood of your project.

Style   This is the most difficult element to define since style is an interpretation of your own creativity. However, as you progress with the craft, you will soon develop a style that is recognizable. Your choice of colors, blooms and themes will result in a unique composition. There are a number of recognized styles which you can aim for initially. Some of the most popular include the country look, in which simplicity of color and form achieves a naive charm; the romantic look, in which soft pastel colors and pretty combinations of shapes create feminine

Opposite: Some species, such as this blue larkspur, look spectacular used alone. When selecting flowers for this style of composition make sure the fresh specimen is perfect in every detail and press several so that you have a margin for error.

This delightful idea was created for a baby's nursery and the color
Make sure you have a good selection of pressed materia

...and flowers include miniature rose buds and forget-me-nots.
...on hand when starting work on a composition.

appeal; the natural look, in which wild flowers are arranged the way that they appear in nature; and finally, the lush and exotic look, which defies convention (and nature) with its completely individual combinations of colors and blooms.

FINISHING TECHNIQUES

Once you have decided on a composition, you must then arrange it on the chosen background and secure it in place. Make sure you have all the necessary equipment on hand. Take all possible precautions to avoid interruptions.

Place a quantity of glue in a shallow dish so it is easy to use. Rubber-based glue is good as it does not dry as quickly as clear glue. Then, using tweezers or forceps, carefully lift each bloom. Use an orange (manicure) stick to dab a small amount of glue on the center of the underside, choosing the stalk, stem, or strongest part of the plant. Avoid placing glue in the middle of delicate petals where it may show through; work with the center of the tip instead.

Continue to lift each specimen in turn, applying glue and replacing the flower carefully on the background. You may find it useful to apply a thin layer of rubber-based glue to the background paper itself in the shape of your arrangement.

Using scissors, trim any excess pieces of stalk or leaf. With a small brush, remove excess bits and pieces of plant material. Excess glue should be removed immediately. Too much glue can dry to a shiny blob on your work.

Fixing your arrangement in place requires care and patience more than any particular

skill. The procedure will be time consuming at first, but as you become more adept at handling the pressed specimens, you will gradually become faster. Once you have fixed all the plant material in place, allow the

1. Move the pressed flowers around on the background until you are happy with their position.

4. Replace the flower on the background, taking care not to smudge glue.

composition plenty of time to dry. Store it carefully, away from drafts, in a warm, dry place, out of any direct sunlight. Once a pressed flower picture is thoroughly dry (test it by moving the whole piece very gingerly,)

it is ready to be framed.

Note: The finished composition will be quite dry, very brittle and easily damaged, so take care when storing the work or transporting it to the framer.

2. Fix the larger specimens in place first.

3. Apply glue with an orange (manicure) stick to center underside of the flower.

5. Trim away excess plant material from the edges of the picture.

6. Use tweezers or forceps to move the smaller blooms into position.

BEGINNER'S PROJECT

THE MOST POPULAR of all pressed flower projects are pressed flower pictures. The range of possibilities is infinite and may eventually surpass the hanging space on your walls. Pictures can be of any size, from miniatures to large collages, creating all sorts of decorative effects.

Posies and bouquets

Arrangements which follow familiar floral shapes such as the posy or bouquet make an excellent starting point for a pressed flower picture. The theme can be based on color, the seasons, or you can press blooms from a special-occasion posy or wedding bouquet to turn into a souvenir pressed flower picture. You can aim for a simple effect such as a summer posy created from pressed daisies, cornflowers and baby's breath, or a luxurious bouquet featuring lilies for a more formal design.

Wreaths and garlands

Because these have a definite form, a little more discipline is required in creating them. The look is a romantic one and calls for soft colors and a good mix of specimens, from open flowers to buds. At the beginning, it will help if you draw the outline of your shape in pencil on the background paper. Use a compass to draw the circular outline required for a wreath. As a finishing touch, you can add a bow of narrow, satin ribbon to the completed picture. Be precise in the arrangement of the blooms and aim to let a little of the background material show through between the flowers to prevent the picture from becoming too heavy. Specimens which have a natural curve will work to your advantage and each bloom should be carefully positioned with the finished shape in mind.

Herbals and samplers

Herbals and botanical compositions are based on the traditional lists and drawings used by herbalists and botanists thousands of years ago. Their simple form is appealing. Some botanical compositions rely on a single plant meticulously reconstructed and labeled. Others require a series of plants which are arranged in ordered rows. Simple plants are the best choice. Garden herbs, wild flowers, or "cottage garden" species can all be used effectively. It is a good idea to press at least three of the individual specimens you plan to use, that way you will be assured of a margin for error. When working with a series of plants such as you might find in a true herbal, keep a careful eye on the balance of your composition and take care not to let any one specimen dominate the picture. If the plants are to be labeled, make sure there is enough room on the background paper. A floral sampler imitates its cross-stitch counterpart. It can be composed on a seasonal theme – a spring sampler for example – or as a personal record of your own favorite flowers. Again, this formalized type of composition offers a special challenge and you will need to

A selection of simple, "cottage garden" plants in creams and yellows has been used to fashion this pretty heart. Lightly pencil in the shape on the background paper and place the largest blooms in position first. Flowers with a natural curve will help to create the correct shape.

be exact in selecting flowers for size and scale as well as color and form. When working with a single specimen plant, select small, compact species for best results.

Baskets and collages

The starting point for a basket composition is the basket itself.

There are several ways of doing this: one is to cut out a basket shape from a material such as flat woven cane which can be bought by the yard. Use a pattern cut from heavy posterboard for the outline and attach it securely to the background paper.

Another method is to create a basket from dried grasses, woven together, then glued and cut to shape. A similar effect can be achieved using pressed fern fronds carefully glued onto posterboard cut into a basket shape.

You could use brown or green postercard or fabric beneath your "basket" for a more realistic effect. Once in place, work from the top of the basket and arrange your pressed flowers to form the outline of the finished shape, then fill in the center.

A pressed flower collage is the least disciplined of all the pictorial compositions. Themes can be inspired by color, the time of year, your own property, or perhaps the forest. A collage can be dramatic, romantic, simplistic or luxuriant. Try various combinations of color and texture, mix unusual shapes and sizes and add obscure or rare species for an exotic effect.

The element of dimension is an interesting one to experiment with. Try placing tall, spiky blooms in the foreground, fading to a distant mass of smaller flowers behind. Non-plant material can be added for an individual look: tiny beads, feathers, little sea shells and ribbon all work well.

Pressed flower stationery

Using pressed flowers to personalize greeting cards and notepaper is a delightful idea and it is always appreciated by the recipient. You can purchase blank cards and heavy weight notepaper, or you can make your own.

First, cut the card to the required size. With the card flat, carefully make an arrangement of pressed blooms and glue these into place. Protect the work with a sheet of blotting paper and place a flat weight such as book on top until glue has dried thoroughly.

There are any number of ideas for decorating stationery; single specimens are simple to work with on this small scale, or you could make a series of cards all featuring the same plant or arrangement. Tiny posies and wreaths can be added to the center of a card, or a single rosebud and leaf in the top corner of notepaper creates a charming effect. Add a finely drawn border and hand-lettering, or create a cameo shape by arranging the blooms on an oval of fabric which has been glued to the center of the card.

Pressed flower decoration

Side tables and jewelry boxes and many other items can be decorated in this way. For the beginner, smaller objects such as little papier-mâché boxes or a wooden photograph frame, make pleasing projects. First insure the surface of the item to be decorated is smooth. If necessary, sand it lightly with fine-grained sandpaper. Select the flattest pressed material, arrange it and secure in place using craft glue.

To protect the surface, several coats of clear varnish should be applied. As this can alter the colors of some pressed flowers, experiment with blooms and varnish on a sheet of paper before starting work.

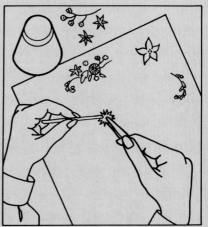

Personalize your own stationery by decorating it with pressed flowers. Here a selection of small-scale blooms has been used to create attractive and distinctive notepaper.

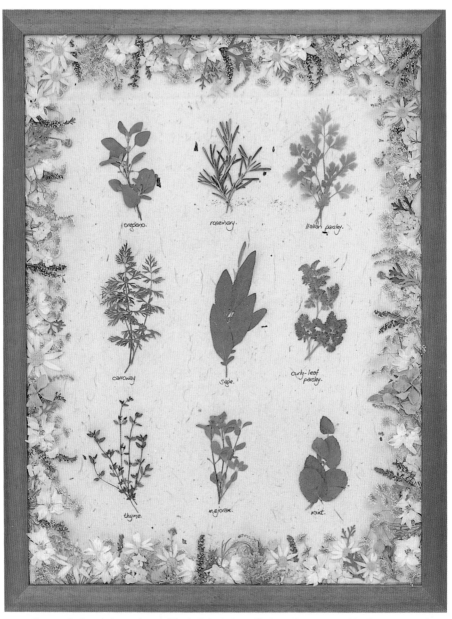

The simple form of a traditional herbal such as might have been created by botanists and herbalists thousands of years ago, has a perennial charm. You can create one like it by following the instructions on the opposite page.

A COUNTRY-STYLE HERBAL

Designed by Catherine Lawrence of
Forget-me-Not Floral Designs

This delightful, country-style herbal makes an ideal beginner's project. It is based on a combination of familiar pressed flowers and garden herbs. The nine pressed herbs have been labeled and then "framed" within a border of pressed flowers and leaves based on a color scheme of cream and green. Handmade paper has been used for the background and the finished composition has been framed with a simple timber frame without a mount.

STEP-BY-STEP DIRECTIONS

MATERIALS

You will need:

1   piece handmade or similar paper 16 x 20 inches
1   piece lightweight posterboard 16 x 20 inches
    Plain timber frame cut to fit.

Pressed Plant Material:

9   different herbs:
    ITALIAN PARSLEY AND CURLY-LEAF PARSLEY, OREGANO, ROSEMARY, CARAWAY, SAGE, THYME, MARJORAM AND MINT.

8   different cream/green flowers and leaves:
    QUEEN ANNE'S LACE (WILD CARROT), GUELDER-ROSE, ASTILBE, WHITE LARKSPUR, THRYPTOMENE, VERBASCUM, HYDRANGEA, FORGET-ME-NOT AND PLAIN AND VARIEGATED IVY LEAVES.

Note: The choice of herbs and flowers may be varied according to availability or individual preference.

STEP ONE

Glue the background paper to the posterboard. Allow to dry.
Form a border right around the edge of the paper approximately 1 1/2 inches wide using the Queen Anne's Lace laid on its side as shown overleaf .
Glue in place.
Make the edge neat by trimming excess plant material with scissors.

STEP TWO

Fill in the border by adding layers of the other flowers and ivy leaves.
Place the largest specimens first and fill in any gaps with the smaller flowers.
Place the smallest flowers, the forget-me-nots, last.
Glue in place.

Step One (see overleaf): Create the floral border first.

Step Three (see below): Arrange pressed herbs in rows of three.

STEP THREE

Arrange the pressed herbs in three rows of three in the following order:

ROW 1	OREGANO	ROSEMARY	ITALIAN PARSLEY
ROW 2	CARAWAY	SAGE	CURLY-LEAF PARSLEY
ROW 3	THYME	MARJORAM	MINT

Glue in place.

STEP FOUR

Label each of the herbs as shown, using a fine marker pen.
Allow to dry and frame to suit.

The finished project in its simple frame makes an ideal picture for a
country-style kitchen or informal dining room.

INDEX